LIGHTHOUSE

A Journal of New Writing

Issue 4 Winter 2013/14

Contents

Gatehouse Press

Published by
Gatehouse Press Limited
90 Earlham Road
Norwich NR2 3HA
www.gatehousepress.com

ISBN 978-0-9928573-0-1

About *Lighthouse*

Lighthouse is a quarterly magazine from Gatehouse Press dedicated to publishing the very best new writing emerging from the UK. It is staffed by voluntary editors and all profits go back into publishing. See editorial for more details.

The typeface for this magazine, IM Fell English, was produced by Igino Marini, and is reproduced with his kind permission: http://iginomarini.com

The *Lighthouse* image was designed and printed using lino cut techniques by Gini Hanbury: http://ginihanbury.blogspot.co.uk

Special thanks to Lee Seaman, James Higham and Ian Buck.

Illustrations by Ben Thompson
Cover design by Norwich Designer
Printed and bound in the UK

Editorial

The False Bride: Folk Songs, Poems, and Ballads

Meirion Jordan and Andrew McDonnell

Meirion:

When we first talked about how we'd like to put this issue together our conversations were continually drawn to the relationship between music and poetry. With things like Robin Robertson's *Hirta Songs* recently released, we thought it was a good angle to take. We're also both fairly active musicians with tastes leaning distinctly towards folk and trad music, so it made some kind of sense to start from that perspective. At some point along the way Andy mentioned the ballad of The False Bride, which is this rather moody, obsessive song about a jilted lover. But as we talked about it more and more that particular ballad started to draw in some of our thoughts on what we like about poetry, its relationship to music, and how the differences between contemporary 'art' poetry and ballad poetry raise questions for contemporary writers.

Andrew:

I first heard the song 'The False Bride' on Alasdair Roberts' early solo record, *The Crook of My Arm* (2001), an intimate affair of songs he has obvious affection for. Released on the indie label Secretly Canadian, the LP was surprising and rather lovely, sparse and lo-fi with just Roberts' voice and his guitar; it was full of songs like 'Lowlands', 'As I Came in by Huntley Town', and 'Lord Gregory'. It was much later that I heard Roberts' take on the fourth verse:

> The flowers of the forest, they ask it of me
> How many strawberries grow in the salt sea?
> And I answer them with a tear in my eye,
> How many dark ships sail the forest?

I sometimes have these moments with a record (or a poem), where I've previously missed something and then it strikes you. I think with 'The False Bride' I was driving and suddenly could not believe what I was hearing. There was something so alarming about the juxtaposition of sea and forest, these two liminal spaces. The woods and the sea take on important psychological roles as both hinterland and theatres for dark imaginings. Fairy tales needing a turn will often head into the enchanted forest, just as the ocean offers a handy exile for those having to abandon home and seek a new life. What's interesting to my ear is the image of the dark ship: like Aguirre staring in disbelief at the delicate wooden galleon in the canopy of the forest, it has a deep melancholy, an image that somehow expresses the pain of the voice in The False Bride through startling imagery. With its riddle-like distortions it lifts the song above the mundane and infuses it with an emotional charge and a mystery.

Meirion:

On first hearing that verse I automatically assumed that it was a fragment of colourful language whose context had passed from memory. Perhaps, I thought, it's a hold-over from a now eroded strand of the story, like versions of the 'Lamkin' ballad that omit the verse explaining why Lamkin seeks his bloody revenge on Lord Arnold's family. So I was pretty surprised to learn that the verse is a nineteenth-century interpolation from a Scottish nursery rhyme, whose words replace some of the other, more moralising (and indeed bitterly misogynistic) verses that characterise older versions of the song.

It's a fascinating verse for me because it was added into the song around the time the printed broadsheet ballad was dying out. Alasdair Roberts' version is closely related to the Ewan McColl and Peggy Seeger version, which was itself taken from a Scottish version of the ballad from around 1910. The ballad as a whole is much older (from at least the seventeenth century), but the verse with the 'folk of the forest' is something that seems to have been added in when singers were starting to lose access to the old printed ballads and were having to remember, not always accurately, the versions their parents' and grandparents' generation had sung. So new verses were getting thrown into the mix on a regular basis. For me that sense of creative dismemberment has a lot of attractions: I'd like to see a bit more of it in contemporary poetry, because poetry is one of the few places where I think that does actually work. Poetry shares that unprinted, unprintable, musical side that makes it malleable in the seesawing between a plurality of printed and spoken versions.

Andrew:

Just after starting to write this, I also heard the Shirley Collins version from the sixties (also in the car). Again the verse appears but it's the folk of the forest and the ship is of no discernible hue. I guess one of the joys of interpretation is that we can reappropriate verse in new ways. Don Paterson's *The Eyes* is an interesting reinterpretation of Antonio Machado, which perhaps points to where contemporary poets find room for reappropriating the work of others in a similar way to the collectors and performers of folk songs. One could also look to Robert Lowell's collection *Imitations* (and even the rewriting of his own books), or Peter Scupham's *The Poets Call on the Goddess Echo*, or the poetry of Jack Spicer: there's no shortage of writers who've tried on the voices of other poets to create something new and unique. Paul Stephenson comes to mind with the didactic spirit of Cafavy's Ithaka in his poem 'Wake up and...' from issue #2 of *Lighthouse*, which in turn raises the question of the translator and the pantechnicon of theories that go with it (tackled in the forthcoming *Lighthouse #5*). It's a shame so many of the poets caught up in the recent plagiarising débacle hadn't tried harder with their rewrite - and more importantly, with acknowledgement. It would have at least been an interesting approach.

The modern versions maintain the didactic spirit of 'The False Bride', warning us of the dangers of unreciprocated love, and of obsession, but the song uses a rhetoric more like that of contemporary poetry to speak to us afresh. Roberts has since re-recorded a version with the guitarist RM Hubbert (2012) that plays with the form again, yet keeps the forest verse more or less intact which is interesting in itself.

On the page, the feeling of weight created by that one verse is much more successful to my eye/ear than the slightly overcooked final verse about graves, roses and taking a long sleep. In fact, a modern editor might suggest that a poet stops at the forest verse. But the song needs that closure in a way a poem would not.

Meirion:

I actually have less difficulty with the remaining verses: the snippets about the grave and the roses (or roots, or turfs, or whatever they happen to be in any one particular version) are just another outcropping of a verse that's almost ubiquitous in the tragic ballad repertoire. It defies our modern sense of what constitutes 'good' verse by simply being from another understanding of how to put poetry or lyric together. As Ian Duhig points out in his feature for this issue, the very idea of it makes no sense to a contemporary poetry scene that demands newness, 'excellence' or other buzzwords at every bite. The rise of 'creative writing' as an idea seems to have accelerated our confusion over what it is our creativity is supposed to accomplish.

Looking back at 'The False Bride's mixture of the presciently modern and the unreachably anachronistic I'm drawn to it more and more. There's a real confidence there that the poet/singers involved in its performance aren't merely contributing to their own little piles of glory - their emergence, if you like - but are contributing verses for the benefit of a wider community of singers and listeners. There's a sizeable backlog of writing dealing with this sort of process in contemporary poetry, and indeed Kathryn Gray's detailed exploration of the problems with 'emergence' in our back pages indicates that this isn't just an in-house concern. What else is modern prize-culture, for example, except an attempt to forestall our perceived irrelevance to future generations, to indicate that among all the newness, some of it really did stick?

But it's a problem that, for me, goes back again and again to The False Bride and its willingness to accept both old and new as necessary, revitalising adjuncts to the business of communicating. That puzzling fourth verse was born from the disintegration of the printed ballad-sheet culture, where singers were interpolating new verses freely among the scraps of older ones. It speaks volumes for me that this disintegration of an old print culture produced a spectacular highlight of a new, revived folk idiom: what modern poet would risk the same of their own verse?

Prose and Poetry

Andrew Spragg

Sonnet

cracked pages and several lit in
the middle hours - who can hear
the wrong things all the time
when all there can be is to do

something everything kept long
in the cooling off - just trip it up
trip it up
collision data rewound about

over four
junk
just junk it
shadow about it

sung wolfishly
the hand makes its sense

Cotton and Linen

it explains
itself

packaged distance
looked out
and in the grasses
you saw there

sweat
and watching
between the
tiles

those close
portions
of our
dreams

something is
withheld -
by the concern
of the rail-light

Chris Tracy

Boy

My acorn pocketer, wind chime
tinkler, like magnets they draw you
as we dawdle through the cemetery:
slabs of ice, a haphazard mosaic,

from the butt that fills the vases
of browning graveside flowers.
Inside, yellow petals
might be flies trapped in amber.

You hold them to the light, gasp
like Midas - then laugh
as we smash and scatter them

across the tarmac, each one
leaving a tiny hill of sherbet
to dissolve behind us in the rain.

Vish Amarasinghe

No Ego Proprioception

'So I was backstage, supine on the rug
with my Taylor, unpicking the problem,
while the metal-heads finished up.
No, I couldn't hear myself,
but I've got guitar proprioception.
I solved it, anyway:
the riff was missing the third
in the middle; that's why it sounded
a little stretched. The heavy-metal jocks
wouldn't get it. They got plenty of cheers,
sure, but the crowd don't get it either;
they just dance. It takes a trained ear
to know. I went on late and cleaned up;
the metal-heads scared a few away,
but I left the remainder stunned,
and that's how you do it.
Screw the cheers.'

Ben Thompson, *AdAm* (Evolution Replacement)

Lara Williams

Taxidermy

At twenty-eight, Lydia lost her boyfriend.

At twenty-nine, she lost her job.

At thirty, she lost her hair, all of it, her full head of hair.

Her boyfriend left one Sunday afternoon, an otherwise ordinary Sunday; and so the breakup felt like something perfunctory, some chore he felt obliged to complete, like taking out the bins or finishing the washing up.

I'm leaving you, he said, as they sat on separate sofas, reading the papers, coffee cooling in their laps.

Lydia tore a page from the food and drink supplement, wafting it in his general direction; a coterie of croissants and cake, of biscuits and brioche; the hoodwinking and hairspray, the nulling, gratifying trickery of broadsheet food photography. Chocolate nut cookies, she said. This is what I'm going to bake today.

She put on a coat and went to the shops to buy ingredients: eggs and butter, white chocolate and macadamias. When she got back he'd started packing, the flat partially autopsied, cardboard boxes and gym bags littering the floor. She ignored them, busying herself in the kitchen, melting butter to a sunshine sizzle, swirling eddies of melted chocolate into the mix. She put them in the oven, set the timer for fifteen minutes, then went to the bathroom to be sick. By the time the cookies were ready, he was leaving.

Aren't you going to have a cookie? she said.

Well I suppose I'll have one, he replied, taking one, taking the biggest one, eating it, eating the whole thing standing there in front of her, staring at the gradually pooling tears in the corners of her eyes. Don't cry, he said. One day you will see that this was for the best.

The job followed. She started turning up late, tired, one time, drunk. Still drunk from the night before, wearing an outfit that could only be the sartorial judgement of the still inebriated.

We need to talk, her boss said. About your performance.

I'm sorry, Lydia replied. But I think you've mistaken me for someone who gives a fuck.

And then it was the hair. When the hair started falling out, it seemed almost inevitable, the big reveal, the punchline. Was she even surprised? More perplexed as to why it hadn't happened sooner. After one thing ejected itself from you, the rest, she found, followed.

The hair was, in many ways, the greater loss; at least on a day-to-day level. It was her only indulgence; a single source of vanity, buoyant loops twirling giddily around her shoulders, glossy tendrils hanging like rice noodles. For a time, she wore a wig, but couldn't stand removing it, removing her hair, along with her make-up at night, to slip under the sheets like a big, bald baby. And so she would wrap her head in a silk scarf, sometimes tying it in a knot above her forehead, like a turban, other times fastening it at the nape of her neck, like a low ponytail. Sometimes she would catch a glimpse of herself and think she looked almost elegant, but the thought was fleeting, like a fleck of dust that hangs in the air, impossible to catch.

On her mother's advice, she took up a hobby; taxidermy, enrolling on a course at her local college. Making dead things look nice: there was a poignancy in that, there was a catharsis. She learned to prepare, to stuff, to treat and mount small birds and rodents, wiring their wings into celestial spans, positioning their feet into stances. Her friends would collect roadkill, wrapping them in plastic bags, passing them to her furtively, in artisanal coffee shops. Her freezer was full of them: mice, finches, on a few occasions, hamsters, gifted from her friend Stacie, a primary school teacher who was always forgetting to feed the school pet. She loved her new hobby. It made her feel artistic and wild, a true bohemian, with her bald head and coarse, chemical-calloused fingers. She felt like she had shed layers of herself and gotten to her core, acrid and uncompromising.

She felt great.

On her tutor's suggestion, she started teaching taxidermy, facilitating workshops at a school for marginalised teenagers, their eyes luminescent with audacity and pride.

Look! they would call over to her, giddily displaying their wares: voles in sunglasses, house sparrows in top hats.

She decided to move, wanting somewhere cheaper, somewhere more humble, more manageable, and started renting a room from an elderly couple, on the outskirts of town. It was a small room but it was comfortable; she'd leave the window open at night, feeling the crisp breeze on her naked scalp, the broth-y scent of Terry and Margaret's cooked chicken, carrying from the kitchen. She stopped wearing headscarves.

This is me, she thought. And I have nothing to hide.

Her ex-boyfriend called. He wanted to check up on her, to make sure she was doing okay. He felt bad, he said, about how things had ended.

Oh, but I am great, she said. You were right. About it being for the best.

But the exchange left her cold, wheedling into her heart and head, and she started thinking it might be nice to have somebody again, to have somebody to care about, to have somebody to call.

Would you ever get back together with him? Stacie asked.

Would I? she replied, considering it, turning it over, flipping it upside down like a pancake; a pancake with a hideous underside. Not for, she started. Not for all the tea in China! which was a strange thing to say, for the first time ever.

Leaving her class one evening she balanced an owl she had been working on, on her car bonnet, the wings wired into a dazzling display, her canvas bag jostling utensils at her side. She recognised a man approaching her as one of the teachers she had seen occasionally in the staff room. She thought he was very handsome.

What's this? he asked, raising an eyebrow, hovering at the car parked next to her.

She felt herself blushing, coming over nervous, telling him she taught taxidermy, this was her current project, and she'd brought it in to show her students.

That's cool, he said. She'd never been called cool before. She'd never been called cool even once before. Maybe I'll see you around, he finished, and she giggled and got in her car. Maybe, she replied. Maybe.

She backed up and drove off, watching him reflected in her wing mirror. He was tall and dark, dapper in a maroon chequered shirt, and pointed, brown leather brogues.

He leant against his car and lit a cigarette, watching her until she disappeared down the road. He thought about what pretty eyes she had. What a lovely voice she had. How cool it was that she taught taxidermy. Thinking what a shame, such a damn shame, it was that she had no hair.

Eleanor Perry

From AETHER/NULL

"supple, unuttered just
as you found it
                    lilt
let it remain"

lith of flies each thieve
and likely lapse infleck
stint   ever lied I lied
or seethe
             and song lick

"the tree dies in winter
and lonely   you spoke"

stitch wisp
a clasp   sleet
ah blithersong
withal   a wing
gold shrug scrub
skelet   elm

Francine Elena

Orange Squash

Plastic beaker
full of orange squash,
pass me it; I want
the tang of the church
hall in my throat, the
citric yellow
Fruit of the Loom,
lemon clover
Brownies round
a papery toadstool,
tattered owl and women
in NHS glasses singing
to a shonky piano.
Little stretched fingers
in threes of sixes
making bulky promises.
Quiet imps in pelerine socks
we would lend a hand and
serve tea and sew a tawny
badge to say we had done so.

Matt Howard

A man hit on the head by a falling flowerpot in Rome

On Via *wherever*, right by me,
in the eternal city. There was such blood,
though he was still breathing
when I reached him, wilting
in that August sun, raw enough to fry an egg.

I was alone with an Italian
and couldn't understand. Confessions are hard
in a language you don't know.
Maybe he was saying how he fell
his whole life, or words for a family -

all the time me just willing he could stand,
look at me, laugh, pointing at the flowerpot.
And it would be clear
it was enough to have killed us,
fallen from god knows how far.

Ben Thompson, *Eev* (Evolution Replacement)

Duran Parsi

Hosgeldeniz

when even the sky feels different meaning the clouds here are from a different air
or rather the difference in everything is told by looking up
white barges move leisurely as they've done a thousand times with red-topped houses mish-mashed on a once grassy hill resembling legos
the city wakes up to a crescent moon still visible against the dawn
and you wonder about things like how people drive here or whether the men selling simit on street corners have the same supplier
and strangely everyone speaks english except the old cab drivers who complain about tourists and arabs
and I think to myself that I'm lucky I blend in
everyone here knows their history and where the monuments are and where I live there are no monuments
and young kids here have Ataturk's signature tattooed on their arms and chests and speak passionately because they understand the situation
not like here
I remember the trip from the airport passing through a barren hillside that somehow carried itself proudly
and seeing a flag in the distance and nothing else but a hill and flag and thinking it defined this place perfectly
"I guess you can just take me home now"
I'll go back to the traffic and ignorance and bad food and know that despite all that my life is good
and I'll sometimes hear the morning prayer in my head and think about the summer here

Melissa Diem

Glimpsed Auntie in New York

I'm stuck by another property in the keys   living in Ireland and longing
These days I spend more time imagining lottos and picking out real estate
It's structured
over a dune   a long legged hollowed out animal   on its way to the beach
I had an auntie in New York in the seventies   twirling around such a home
with structured wooden steps running in multiples   up to the house or down
to the shore
and sometime even just to the sides   She has a high-waisted bikini on
oversized sunglass
and Jackie O smile   This is the image I play of my aunt   it must've been the
Hamptons   it must've belonged   to someone else   a sunburst and sparkly
eye opener to a seven year old
girl who secretly wished   she was adopted   but someone arrived and
limbs moved   and my auntie could be heard make sorts of apologises and
explanation
I was wearing culottes and my hair in a bun
My father said - it was typical and something about real world commitment
But my aunt wasn't the one   fleeing New York in a yellow VW beetle
and driving down to Florida

Ben Thompson, *Even With All This Space People Insist On Mooring Together*

Simon Petkovich

Carrots

religiously dan-

gling that litt-
le mirror glass

bead technolo-

gical wonder-
land carrot

Money

1

credit
card-

ace of

tur-
moil

2

the sp-
ent for-

ce of fin-

ance

Jack Reynolds

Compo Proc

I'm late and it's too hot and I'm sweating when Morris finally answers the phone.

'Alright mate? All shipshape and ready to roll?'

He sounds his usual stoned self, apparently unruffled by the five missed calls. I try and sound cool too.

'Yeah. Should be able to do about £200 today.'

'Nicely nice.'

'Listen, Risso, I'm gonna need you to make it 35p on the pound from now on. It's getting risky. My manager's got his eye on me.'

This is not true: Adam never notices anything except lateness or slowness. You could swipe his Homer Simpson tie from under his chin and he wouldn't blink. You could probably put it on yourself as long as you processed enough forms. Morris inhales sharply, fuzzing the line.

'No can do Wezza. I can do 30. They're not that easy to shift you know.'

'Okay. Fair enough. Should hit your doormat in a couple of days.'

'Standard.'

'Yeah. Anyway, I best get off.'

'You better had mate.'

I end the call by pressing the power button on top of the phone - easier and quicker than using the touchscreen. 30p isn't great, but it's better than the 25 I've been getting so far.

The main station clock has no hands, and hasn't for months, maybe years, but the digital readout in the bottom right corner of the '80s vintage departures screen says 15:02, so I'm already two minutes late. Instead of letting us work normal hours, the Company has us processing from 15:00 to 22:00. This pattern mystifies from every angle. The extra cost of lighting the office all evening alone must make it more costly to the Company than a regular 9-5.

The only-slightly-delayed 14:53 arrival from Liverpool Street has just disgorged its passengers onto the platform, and now they're filtering through the automatic ticket barriers, getting in my way and forcing me to trace a curving route to the STAFF ONLY door next to the Budgens Convenience Shop.

The Company installed the ticket barriers to make sure nobody gets away with a fare-dodge, but they've never worked properly - at least, they can only read pristine tickets, not the crumpled things people have in their pockets at the end of a journey - so each one is permanently manned by a flourescent-jacketed security man whose job is to visually check each ticket, then open the barrier by waving a special magnetic open-sesame card in front of a special magnetic detector pad.

When passenger traffic's light, the security men check every ticket, but when big trains come in and new arrivals overrun the gates, they just hold their open-sesames over the detectors and, with unseeing eyes, let the horde stream through, fare-dodgers and all.

It's this kind of inefficiency - along with a lifetime of being personally overcharged by the Company every time I go anywhere - that makes me feel that the whole arrangement with Morris is a right and true thing.

There seems to be a keener than usual absence of gorm amongst today's passengers, and I have to pick my way through slack-faced board-watchers, last-minute suitcase rearrangers and fly-like meanderers who seem unable to comprehend the system they find themselves in.

Despite their best obstructive efforts, I make it to the STAFF ONLY door and tap in the code: 1066X - a good, warlike, British code - and step into the STAFF ONLY region.

A confusion of empty corridors, staircases and doublebacks, this privileged area resembles the digestive system of a gigantic marine animal: walls, ceilings, architraves, doors and frames are all painted in what must be an inch-thick lining of grey gloss, the top layer permanently tacky and glistening.

Up three flights of stairs, the corridor's windows look out over the concourse. If I wasn't late, I'd take a moment to enjoy the feeling of secret power this view always gives me. Instead, I push on past the break room to the door labeled COMPO PROC.

The label is handwritten in Adam's capitalised bubble-lettering, each letter peeking out from behind the last, each a different shade of felt-tip.

I'm only a couple of minutes late, but as soon as I step into the yellowed air of the seedy, never-decorated open-plan office everyone looks up accusingly from the blue blaze of their flatscreens. Advancing under cover of this eyeborne artillery of judgement, Adam tousles the Movember smudge of his top lip with a thumb and forefinger. When he reaches me, he stops and folds his arms.

'Late again, Wesley, late again.'

'Sorry boss, my mum rang while I was walking in and I couldn't get her off the phone.'

'No excuse, Wesley. No excuse at all. I've said before-'

Before he can continue, I jump in.

'Got it. Must do better. Will do better.'

Adam's expression is all exasp and unbelief, and his arms stay folded, but he angles his body slightly so I can pass. The only reason he makes a special fuss when I'm late is because he doesn't want everyone to think that I'm his favourite, just because I'm the best processor.

In my corner, my desk is bare but for the flatscreen, the keyboard and the mouse, which sits on its Company-branded mousemat with its too-cheerful GOING

PLACES!! slogan and abstract-beyond-sense logo, which looks to me like a grinning assassin with one eye closed, drawing a bead on my wallet.

At the desk next to mine, Amber has already logged in and is dividing her stack of forms into piles. She has her own system, which looks hopelessly inefficient to me. The chart by the printer agrees. She smiles at me without taking out her earbuds. Amber's serious and always on time. She's got a boyfriend, but I can tell she likes me by the way she smiles. Judging from her break-room complaints she possibly likes me more than she likes her boyfriend, but I'm not the type to steal someone's girl, so I'm happy with the smiles and the complaints.

I press Ctrl-Alt-Del to bring up the login screen, and tap in my staff ID - TEMP0034 - and my password, which is still 'password,' despite the day-one-training-session mandate to change it.

Just as I slam two fingers down on the return button, Adam appears at my shoulder and dumps a three-inch thick stack of forms on my desk. Most processors get an inch of forms at the start of the shift, but I am not most processors, so Adam always loads me up.

'Let's see if we can't break the record, shall we Wesley?'

He means my record: 287 compensation forms processed in one six-hour shift, nearly double the previous record set by some long-ago temp named Lance, according to the chart.

'I'll see what I can do.'

Adam walks to the centre of the room and addresses the whole office:

'Right, gang, listen up. Come on, listen up everyone!'

The insectoid clicking of mice slows and stops. Amber takes out one earbud.

'We're going to try something new today. No offence to Wesley, but he's not Superman. There's no reason why all of you can't hit 250 per shift, at least.'

He reaches into his pocket and withdraws a blue rectangle the size of a credit card.

'Whoever gets the most done today gets this,'

He holds up the card and presents it to each corner of the office, even the corner taken up by the big printer and the photocopiers.

'A £10 Odeon Gift Card!'

Nobody seems very impressed. At least, nobody makes a sound. Adam's smile waxes wan.

'Just because the trains are slow doesn't mean we have to be. Right - GO!'

The 'GO!' fails to spark anyone's engine, and when the mice start clicking again, it is with the insistent rhythms of Solitaire and Minesweeper, not the slow dance for keyboard and mouse of the Company database.

I take the first form off my pile and get started, copying the information from the box-per-letter form into the empty database record displayed on the flatscreen.

If your train is more than half an hour late, you're entitled to compensation from the Company. For delays of between half an hour and 59 minutes, this compensation amounts to half of the ticket's face value. For delays between one hour and infinity, you get a full refund, although it's only ever paid in Company vouchers, which can only be used to buy more train tickets, and for which no change is given, which is why Morris only pays me a fraction of the face value.

To claim compensation, you have to fill out a form, staple your ticket to it and send it to our office. No ticket, no voucher. Finding the forms is no easy task. At smaller stations they simply don't exist, and at larger ones you have to ask for them; they're never kept in the stands of timetables and special offer leaflets. This manufactured scarcity helps the Company minimise payouts, and gives me extra justification for my arrangement with Morris.

I am the best at entering the forms into the computer. The best that ever was. But I am cheating. The final, and - if you have properly roboticised the most efficient sequence of keyboard shortcuts - most time consuming part of processing a form is entering the train time into a special dynamic field. Once filled, this field checks with another database whether the train was really late, and, if so, whether the claimant has tried to get one over on the Company by claiming a full refund for a 59 minute delay. If they are telling the truth, it displays 'Agreed 10305.' Once this is displayed, the 'Next' button in the lower right of the screen becomes clickable, and you advance to the printing of the vouchers.

The thing is that you can just type 'Agreed 10305' in the box, press return, and the 'Next' button will solidify, bevelled edges darkening from grey to blue, letting you skip the check and its attendant 30 second delay, and advance to the next form. In order to simulate the waiting period, I process every third form covertly, with casual, spiderlike fingerstrokes designed to resemble the patient rocking of a hand waiting for checking to be done.

I'm off to a good start today: ten minutes in and I'm already at eight forms. I believe in my heart that with determination and practice I will one day be able to do a form a minute, but - for now - fifty per hour is a respectable target.

Amber seems to be the only other person in the office tempted by the Odeon Gift Card. She's gargoyled over her keyboard, thrumming her fingers on the desk during the checking process, her right hand moving quickly to the mouse so she can click the Next button. She doesn't know that you can press Tab three times then Return to avoid losing precious seconds to moving your hand, moving the pointer, moving your hand back.

I let muscle memory pull me through the forms, my mind barely ticking over, its only job to relay the names and postal addresses of the claimants to my fingers, until it's 4:00 and I'm 48 forms deep in what looks to be a record-threatening performance. At 50 forms, I lean back in my chair, contort my spine, then dive back in.

By 5:00 I've hit 101, and I decide to reward myself by printing off a voucher for Morris. Morris understandably doesn't want them sent under his real name, so they go to his house addressed to names from books, the real names of rappers or superheroes, whatever is going through my mind. Today they will go to Tenzil Kem, the secret identity of the Matter Eater Lad, last survivor of a starving race who cheated extinction by evolving the ability to metabolise anything - even the superdense material left after a supernova - although I'd like to see him try and get through a Caffe Ritazza egg salad sandwich.

Tenzil Kem's first £75 voucher is worth, according to the Windows Calculator, £22.50 to me, a significant and deserved boost to my hourly rate. I type 'Agreed 10305,' press tab three times, and hit return to seal the deal. Without missing a beat, I go back to the pile of real claims, planning a series of psychic waypoints, significant numbers where concentration can break and I can, for a few moments, remember myself and stop being perfect. The next will be at 150 forms.

At 140 forms it's suddenly dark outside. In the corner of my eye, Adam rises from his desk and moves to the centre of the room.

'Right guys, listen up. I know a tenner at the cinema's not much, but I thought it'd be something. Wesley's nearly a hundred ahead already, and the rest of you are on the go-slow. I thought we were a team. I thought tonight would go down in history.'

He walks to my desk.

'Here you go, Wesley. You've earned it.'

He spits the words, places the bright blue gift card on the corner of my desk and walks away, shoulders heavy, gait laden with doom.

I turn the gift card over in my fingers and savour the play of the light on the metallic Odeon logo, which is just the word ODEON, and does not offend me. Despite the sourness of the air after Adam's announcement and the mutters and jabbing glances aimed at my corner, I feel like the Matter Eater Lad felt on the day he was granted membership to the League of Superheroes.

Adam sits down again. I watch him rub his eyes and perform some internal recombobulation before he goes back to whatever it is he does for five and a half hours a day after handing out the forms.

Exposed to the jealous surveillance of my fellow temps, I abandon my perfect system and go back to the imperfection handed down on training day, in case anyone glimpses my secrets. Amber taps me on the shoulder without taking out either of her earbuds. She unsmilingly mouths 'Well done,' then goes back to her own pile at her usual diligent but unspectacular speed, no longer hunched and urgent. Defeated. By me. Like everyone.

As 7:00 approaches, temps begin to rise in twos and threes and make their way to the break room. Amber's just given me her usual funny, squinting, head-cocking invitation to join her for coffee and boyfriend complaints when Adam once again appears in the middle of the room.

'Hold it everyone. Dean, can you call the rest back in here?'

Dean, a vertiginously-coiffed and skinnily-jeaned temp, pauses in the act of stepping through the breakroom door, and summons the breakers back into the office. Everyone looks to Adam.

'New rule, everyone. Company says every voucher worth more than £50 has to be approved by me. Once you've put it through, drop the form and the ticket on my desk, and I'll OK the vouchers for printing. Any big ones you've already done today, go through your piles and bring them to me.' He gives the room a quick, strafing look of command, re-energised by his new orders.

'Thanks, gang.'

My neck goes limp and my head flops forward. I am a thief. I am a thief, and everyone will know that I am a thief. There's no form for Tenzil Kem's claim, no ticket, only the digitally-encoded certainty that his claim was processed by my user account.

I am a thief, and I will be punished like a thief. I am not a hero like the Matter Eater Lad. I will never save the Earth.

Amber gives me the squinty head-cock again. I expend my entire store of nonchalance on a shake of the head and go back to work, or - truthfully - to staring at the screen while my braincells move to freakout stations and hurl recriminations at one another.

A hundred and fifty forms seems a long way off, but after a minute of staring, the guilty cells have been corralled by the devious, and a plan has formed. I am a thief, but I am not a thief who gets caught.

The first thing is to surreptitiously slide one of Amber's pre-sorted sheafs over to my desk. This done, I flick through until I find a £75 First-Class single from here to Liverpool Street matching Tenzil Kem's journey, then unpick the staple and deftly slip the ticket under my keyboard, ready for the next phase.

I return Amber's pile, stand, and walk past the breakroom and out into the grey gloss gullet of the station. I will save you, Matter Eater Lad, I think to myself and choose not to unravel.

I jog down the corridors and stairwells until I burst out onto the concourse. Being careful to stay close to the wall in case anyone happens to see me from the office window, I make my way to the Customer Service Kiosk.

The fat, milky-faced Customer Service man frowns when I push through the glass doors. His badge says his name is Derek.

'Can I have a delay repay form?'

'No delays today, son. You missed your train?'

'It's not for today or for here. My mum got stranded at Somerleyton for an hour last week.'

'No delays on that line this month. It's her fault if she missed it.'

Derek takes a leaflet from the rack behind him and slides it conspiratorially over the Customer Service counter.

'Here's a timetable for the Lowestoft line. Tell your mum to make sure she's there ten minutes early next time.'

For Derek, the conversation is over. There's no-one else waiting, so he's got nothing to do, but he does it busily, fiddling with things behind the counter and eyeing the miniature Departures board on his wall-mounted monitor like it's a pot about to boil.

I turn to walk away, just as salvation shuffles into the Customer Service Kiosk. An old lady, standard-issue quilt coat, shopping basket and unstoppable heartbeat, approaches the desk.

I start again.

'Yeah, can I have a Delay Repay form please? My nan got stranded and she asked me to pick one up for her.'

Derek gives me a Grand-Masterful arch of the eyebrows, but squanders his move:

'Your nan, eh?'

'Yeah. My nan.'

I engage the old lady with a smile. She returns it, leaving Derek the odd man out. I egg the pudding:

'They don't have them at her station, and she doesn't come into town much.'

The old lady turns her smile to Derek, who breaks quickly, as I knew he would.

'Alright, son.'

He reaches into a desk drawer and pulls out a leaflet-folded Delay Repay form, the sniperish Company logo leering menacingly above the gross cowardice and total justification of the 'Compliments and Suggestions' heading.

Down, but not out, Derek looks me in the eye as I pluck the form out of his pinched fingertips. I smile at the old lady again, and make my exit.

Form in hand, I slink back along the wall, through 1066, back through the bowels of the beast and through to COMPO PROC. I'm back at my desk before Amber's finished her coffee break.

Quickly but precisely, I fill in the form on behalf of Tenzil Kem, then pierce it with the levered-open staple still attached to Amber's ticket, closing its sharp little arms with the pad of my thumb. The form looks good, looks real, looks like salvation for the whole planet.

The only thing left is the RECEIVED date stamp in the lower left of the form. This is done by whoever receives the forms, and its presence will ensure the preservation of my secret identity.

There's a date stamp in Adam's desk somewhere, which he uses to stamp the date on our timesheets so we can hand them in at the temp agency, but no easy way to get to it. Adam seems to live on Chunky Kit Kats and apples, which he eats at his desk. Even if he did leave for long enough, I couldn't just go and rifle his drawers in front of the other temps.

I tuck the Tenzil Kem form in at the bottom of my pile. If it weren't for the New Rule, I reckon I'd have got to 300 tonight. There's only another thirty or so left in the first batch.

A ragged bud of inspiration blooms.

I fire into the forms in a transcendent display of my perfect system. Digits twitch, striking true every time, each third form is a miracle of stealth, and I don't even want to waste instants looking at the time, so close do I feel to the form-a-minute dream.

When I get to Tenzil Kem, I pick up the pile of completed forms and set it down on top of him.

I walk over to Adam's desk, where Adam sits in a post-incentive-failure funk.

'All done. Got any more?'

'You've already won the card, you know.'

'I'm going for the record.'

Adam gives me a marvelous look as he revivifies: the warm, wide-eyed look of an appreciative everyday citizen of a newly-saved world. He seems about to say something, but instead just shakes his head and clicks his tongue in delight. He swivels in his chair to face the bales and boxes of forms that are stacked four-high along the wall.

As soon as I'm out of the cone of his vision, my right hand embarks on a special forces operation: while the rest of me stands patiently at ease, waiting for my new forms, my hand slides open Adam's drawer and begins a fingertip scan of the shapes, surfaces and textures within.

The bulbous plastic handle of the date stamp is cool to the touch. Possibly it is ceramic. Either way, as soon as it is detected, the stamp is mine, and it goes in my pocket while I nudge the drawer closed with my hip, just as Adam swivels back with cuckoo-clock timing and a three-inch thick sheaf of forms in his lap.

'This should get you to 300. Oh yeah-'

He clicks on a toolbar button that doesn't appear on my database screen. Tenzil Kem's name appears, next to the date of his claim and the amount of compensation, at the head of a list labelled Outstanding Case Files.

'I need to approve this one. Can you bring it over before you get started?'

Adrenaline from the date stamp liberation answers for me.

'Sure thing. I'll have a look through the pile. Take it easy.'

I never say things like 'Take it easy,' but I seem to have got away with it. Adam closes the Outstanding Case Files window, and I head back to my desk, drop off the forms, and make a beeline for the toilet.

In the grey gloss sanctuary of the Staff Only toilet, I sit on the closed lid of the loo and adjust the date stamp. It's self-inking, but of an old design - unnecessarily intricate, with all sorts of little cogs and springs. I have to look down the end to see the date to be printed, which appears in reverse, while the adjustment wheels are on the other side, making the setting of the date a slow, awkward fiddle.

I actually sigh with actual relief when the right date rolls into view, and I feel too dizzy to stand. After a few deep breaths I flush the toilet and wash my hands for the sake of verisimilitude. I feel myself getting internally tougher and more resourceful with every covert operation. I would make a very good spy.

Back at my desk, I subtly engineer the stamp into the sleeve of my shirt, and swiftly, confidently, with perfect purpose stamp the date in the box in the bottom right corner of the form.

The stamp is already back in my pocket and I've begun to evaluate potential abandonment areas for it when I see the date:

79 October 7568

I am a thief, and I will hang.

Somewhere in the black of my heart, Matter Eater Lad chokes on a fishbone: In Amber's pile is a genuine claim for £75 compensation, to a genuine person delayed, left to grind their soul against a platform for between an hour and infinity.

I have crossed a line. I am not a clever Robin Hood-style thief any more. I am the bad kind of thief. I may as well have stolen £75 from this genuine person's pocket. And I will be caught. The form is useless, a clear fake, and there's no time to get a replacement. Derek certainly won't be keen to give me another.

There is a police station within the train station, connected to this room. It's the British Transport Police, but still, my crime is a British Transport crime, so they're bound to have jurisdiction. Maybe they even have special powers. There will be a heavy, nerve-pinching hand on my shoulder. It will march me through unexplored grey regions to some special internal entrance to the British Transport Police Station. No one will see me go in. I will never be let out.

Without quite deciding to, I rise from my chair and walk out into the corridor, trancelike through the grey gloss guts and out onto the nearly empty concourse. I am about to be furious with myself when I realise I have given myself a head start. This way I won't be collared at my desk, this way I get away. I live with a different set of consequences: I will go to another place and be a bad thief there too. I will steal to survive. This is clearly what I have chosen.

I walk purposefully up to the security barrier at the end of platform 4. The Security Man stops me.

'Need to see all tickets.'

I check my pockets like I'm expecting to find something, then, halfway through my performance, I realise I have left my bag, with my wallet, my phone, my keys - everything - under the desk. I check my pockets for real. All I have is the Odeon Gift Card. Like all thieves, I play the hand I've been dealt.

'I haven't got a ticket. If you let me through I'll give you this.'

I hold out the Odeon Gift Card. The Security Man takes it, looks at both sides, pockets it.

'Sorry mate, didn't hear that. Can I see your ticket?'

I laugh, suddenly and too much: whoever stamps the forms must make a mistake sometimes. I am a thief and a fool, but all is not lost.

I jog back to the 1066 door, through the grey labyrinth, and back into

COMPO PROC.

At my desk, I realise I should've reset the stamp before coming in. It already looks like I've gone to the toilet twice in ten minutes. Another trip will be suspicious and creepy.

Instead, I boldly slip the stamp out of my pocket and steal a look at it under the desk. Immediately, I see my mistake. There, plain to see, a rectangular reticule, right next to the adjustment wheels. The self-inking mechanism makes everything rotate when you stamp, so when you press down, the whole thing spins round before it prints the date.

Hiding the stamp between my legs, I lick the pad of my thumb and smudge the date on the form, but all I succeed in doing is darkening the whole area, making it look very definitely like someone has tried to rub the date off.

I risk a few moments' tinkering with the date stamp, holding it under the desk while I dial the right date into the reticule, trying to look like I'm sending a surreptitious text.

Hands still under the desk, I press the stamp slowly into my palm, then draw my left hand out for inspection. The date is right, so once again I take the stamp into my sleeve, and press down on Tenzil Kem's form, twice this time: once directly on top of the first, terrible attempt, and once slightly above it, at a jaunty 'Oops, silly me!' angle.

Emboldened, I flick through my new sheaf until I find a claim for £66, and quickly process it, making sure I even do the proper checking procedure, in case it turns out to be a false claim. The second I hit Next, I take Tenzil Kem and his £66 partner over to Adam's desk.

'Here you go. Couple of big ones for you.'

Adam looks at the forms, gives a porcine grunt-nod of recognition and clicks the special Supervisor's tab again. With two decisive clicks, Tenzil Kem is legitimised.

I suppress a hoot of pure joy, and return to my desk. There will be no British Transport Police, no eternity in a grey gloss cell. I look at Amber and smile. She smiles back.

My victory is total, though from now on I'll only be able to send Morris vouchers of less than £50, which means four phantom forms per shift instead of three. No significant change to the system, just an order of subdivision. Plus, who knows, maybe dividing the shifts into quarters instead of thirds will help me reach form-a-minute intensity.

One day, I will eat the sun.

James Coghill

Nine-Banded Armadillo

Each morning the same rawness:
the dawn grinding up against my face
and the cracked-glass sky, fretting.

I tell myself this won't be the end of me.

Armadillos do great things too
given time, given speedy recovery,
given appropriate support,

a cure for leprosy

which is the first problem I come to
as I patrol the bounds of my territory,
slowly turning the colour of rotten fruit,

my armour loose as old, stiff bandages.

Towards noon, I dig a shallow hole
to rest in. As luck would have it,
I tap into the root of a termite's nest

and eat my fill before leaving.

It's almost dusk. I meet it
urgently, though I don't know why.
Even the world must move aside.

Manuela Moser

Adele

1886–1921

Out of the darkness the left side of your face comes into view.
There's a shadow of a cheekbone, an outline of your mouth.
A face you grew into while your brothers were in battle
and you were learning the numbers at Georg Fromberg & Co.
where the counting out of bank notes numbered your days.

The contours of your body prove challenging. You refused
the automated privacy of bathing machines. Stripping off
shoes and stockings on the sand, confirming grit to sweat
and shaking off your dress beneath a towel to walk straight
into the sea until suspended by salt. You took baths regularly.

At 21 you fell in love and spent the time avoiding your father.
You planned meetings in places with locks on the doors.
When you couldn't sleep you pushed grey thread through a needle,
embroidered *A.L. A.L. A.L.* onto linen. In the mornings
you often found the letters embedded in your fingertips.

For years you hid the bed sheets and the handkerchiefs
in the tin trunk underneath your bed. You turned the key
for the last time when you heard of his escapades in a hansom.
It left you on the balcony, your father's pistol from your dresser
unthreading each embellishment, initials stained in red.

Imogen Forster

On the Ouse Washes

Grey flannel cloud
sky notched at the horizon
by two asymmetrical towers.

This cathedral -
boundary squatter
inshore platform
humming silo
control tower
launch pad -
this mystery.

Features

Ian Duhig

The Ballad and the Folk

Andrew Duncan in his *Angel Exhaust* 'Hand list of late 20th Century Poets' wrote of me: 'His third book The Lammas Hireling (2003) showed a new admiration for folk styles which chased out literary interest almost altogether.' Reading this in 2010 gave me a good laugh and this isn't an exercise in score-settling - I went on to include Duncan in my list of important Leeds poets for McCann's Tristrapedia-like *How Leeds Changed the World.* Nevertheless, it does express a view of folk culture in a time that fetishizes the innovative. Must good literature necessarily be groundbreakingly original, Terry Eagleton asks in his recent *How To Read Literature*; if so, he points out, 'we would be forced to deny the value of a great many literary works, from ancient pastoral and medieval mystery plays to sonnets and folk ballads'. I'd also draw attention to Kenneth Goldsmith's 'Uncreative Writing' project, with its wholesale and unmediated appropriations of pre-existing texts. Sina Queyras posted an article recently by Kathryn Mockler pertinently asked how truly creative we can be in the modern world. Does a quasi-scientific notion of continual progress really apply to the arts? I recall Michael Longley saying that while music changed after Bach, it didn't necessarily get any better. Every generation overvalues its own products' quality and originality. John Cooper Clarke's 'Chickentown' is very well-known - here's some of it:

> the fucking pies are fucking old
> the fucking chips are fucking cold
> the fucking beer is fucking flat
> the fucking flats have fucking rats
> the fucking clocks are fucking wrong
> the fucking days are fucking long
> it fucking gets you fucking down
> evidently chicken town

Lyrics © John Cooper Clarke, as they say. Is this really so original and different from the following passage in an 'anonymous' (Hamish Blair?) WWII song?

This fucking town's a fucking cuss
No fucking trains, no fucking bus
And no one thinks of fucking us
In fucking Orkney.

The fucking folk are fucking mad
The fucking roads are fucking bad
Good night the bright is fucking sad
In fucking Orkney.

The fucking things are fucking dear
A fucking bob for a fucking beer
And is it good? No fucking fear
In fucking Orkney.

The fucking dances make you smile
The fucking bands are fucking vile
It only cramps your fucking style
In fucking Orkney.

There was a time when the link between poetry and song seemed broken, when Walcott could lament the fact, as he saw it, that 'the concept of song' had gone out of poetry altogether, but both Paul Muldoon and Glyn Maxwell have written perceptively on this subject in the past few years. It's always been the case in Ireland that good poets have written poetry with specific traditional music in mind, such as Padraic Colum and Patrick Kavanagh. Hamish Henderson frequently bridged this so-called divide in Scotland, while Paul Henry is an excellent contemporary Welsh poet who profits from the inherent musicality, in his view, of Celtic languages and literature. It still seems to me that a large proportion of the styles in which poetry is being written now are closer to music than to prose, though we should also remember that there are presently at least as many ways of making music as there are of making poetry: cross-fertilisations happen more easily between fields than within them. I have worked several times with the avant-garde composer Christopher Fox, and with the pre-Baroque music specialists, the Clerks. When they commissioned me to update the Fauvel cycle, it was useful sometimes to give its irregularly-stressed octosyllabic lines a more predictable rhythm in consideration of a modern audience (though I would like to sidestep here the complex issue of syllabic poetry's aural detectability, which is an argument far from being settled within contemporary poetry). This is also more a *traduttore traditore* betrayal than it might sound, as to the medieval listener regular rhythms could sound secular, not to say impure, and inappropriate when the subject matter was spiritual.

Writing in 'folk' traditions is even more obviously an impure activity (I am reminded of that Neruda editorial 'Towards an Impure Poetry' in the Spanish journal *Caballo verde para la poesía*) inevitably suspect to scholars and literary purists. Ballads easily transmit radical politics, which is why they have always been attractive to authors like Brecht, and, at a much lower level, I have attempted the form for that very reason. In terms of its political impact, grandiose claims have been made on behalf of Cambridge poetry's political impact, which were examined then largely demolished by Robert Archambeau in his essay 'Public Faces in Private Places'. Although in a Guardian interview Martin Carthy said, 'I regard tradition as progressive, and a traditional song as a progressive force', in truth it would be hard to identify a significant political impact of any song or poem except to keep up the morale of the troops, as it were. Even then, that might not be particularly admirable: consider Njegoš's epic *The Mountain Wreath* of 1846, a celebration of ethnic cleansing which apparently heartened the Serbs during the Bosnian War of the 1990s. I think it would be an error to imagine folklore keeps alive any lost ancient knowledge forgotten elsewhere, a mirror-image of overvaluing the new. Academic studies of folklore regularly debunk as 'fakelore' many traditions claiming great antiquity which turn out to be Victorian or even more recent inventions; this can apply to songs as well, where disputes over authenticity go back to those surrounding Ossian at least, and probably further. In light of recent scandals about plagiarism, therefore, I was interested to read in Dave Arthur's biography of Bert Lloyd how he was embroiled in so many controversies in this very area, from changing Reynardine's shining eyes to shining teeth through to inventing sources for his versions of songs. Lloyd and his contemporaries (as Macpherson before him) were doing the reverse: passing off their work as other people's, and often imaginary people at that.

Such polyphonic ventriloquism has features in common with Conceptual writing, though it also reflects medieval practices: when I was working on the Fauvel cycle, I was surprised at the relaxed attitudes to authorship normal in fourteenth-century France. Dillon in her 'Medieval Music-Making and the Roman de Fauvel' writes: 'While the deconstruction of the author is most famously associated with a strand of modern critical theory ... medieval texts were extraordinarily inventive in their modes of authorial representation and self-representation, authorial presences were meaningful only insofar as they were deployed within the textual frame.' Contrafacta and the reworking of material (*remaniement*) was normal, as were interpolations and continuations of texts where they were left off by the original writer. This mirrors how folk songs survive and change, particularly in relation to the ballad, where Causley compared its jump-cut technique to film, with each verse a frame. The self-contained nature of ballad verses meant boring ones could easily be dropped over repeated performances, with new verses interpolated to lend excitement to a battle-scene or tenderness to love-affairs - or simply getting rearranged and/or forgotten. For all the world it reminds me of B. S. Johnson's *The Unfortunates*, by my side as

I write this, where, provided the first and last sections are in place, those between them can be shuffled like a deck of cards.

None of this sits easily with modern notions of poets clearly responsible for texts, even where that means appending their names to other peoples' words. Nor does contemporary poetry easily entertain a written ballad's ghostly presence of music in the sense that Dillon describes 'how, in the framework of the book, song operates differently from its sonic realization.' Many people don't appreciate sonic realizations that seem crude beside, say, Schubert's Lieder, though his setting of Goethe's poetry is clearly a distant relative of what I have been describing. Margaret Barry's rendition of Victorian songs doesn't so much revitalize them as give them dimensions they never had in the first place, as in Rilke's translations of Louise Labé's poetry. Perhaps folk music only ever exists in something like a translator's flux, forever between worlds. Yet in the face of all charges of crudity, traditional music can be analysed by its adherents with a subtlety completely absent from much contemporary poetry criticism. You could talk about Roscommon, Kerry and West Limerick *bodhrán* styles and aficionados would know exactly what you were talking about while binary divisions of poetry that are supposed to apply to the whole Anglosphere are routinely peddled in and out of the academy.

There is a larger question behind all this which I can do little more than introduce then dismiss, as the word count hangs over me like a Jedburgh axe. I was reading an interview with the artist Richard Long where he declared 'every artist is a local artist'. What immediately sprang to mind was a remark by a Faber poet who I won't name that 'you can call me any kind of poet you like except a local poet.' Regional (like class) awareness barely features in contemporary poetry. I think of Norman Nicholson, whose poetry lies behind Andy Goldsworthy's marvellous 'The Wall that Went for a Walk'. What happened to Auden's 'A poet's hope to be, like some valley cheese, local, but prized elsewhere'? I suspect what has happened is that it is now considered fatally unsophisticated (worst of offences to current taste) to care what your valley thinks about your work, if it thinks about your work at all. And whose fault is that? It seems like a reasonable question, and I get fed up with people blaming the schools. What about the overwhelming proportion of English Literature graduates who never look at a book of contemporary poetry after they graduate? I have just finished writing an article for another magazine about the poet who is most local to me in terms of where I live in Leeds, the nearly-forgotten and long out-of-print John Riley, who Leeds University doesn't even bother to mention in their 'map' of the city's poetry. I defy anybody to read Riley's *Czargrad* (available in Tuma's Oxford anthology) and say he is a writer of limited horizons. I could listen to Darach Ó Catháin, who many people, including Ciaran Carson, consider the greatest *sean-nós* singer of his generation, in the pub down the road; I could notice Pearse Hutchinson, translator from Galician and Catalan, friend of Catalan poets such as Salvador Espriu and Carles Riba, entranced at another table.

To these questions, as to the other issues I have raised and glanced at here, I have no conclusions or discoveries to offer, only the hope that my enthusiasm for and interest in them is communicable to some of you reading this, even if that interest isn't literary.

Agnes Lehoczky

November Short-Cut

meet you in the Stag tonight the anonymous text read a short-cut through winter via Frog Lane an alley that exists on the map only if you dare doubt it if you venture into that province render yourself invisible so that you stand out in other words a poor aporia unremember the mausoleums of Sharrow and the mouldy micro-climate of their rooms corners congested with hooded muggers concealed rivers dirty vans parked in the same spot forever because they say that something quick a rushed tête-à-tête an agile clause an ad hoc desire to converse failed and stuck in air repeats itself in the pattern of graffitied streets chequered rooftops soot-skinned firewalls drifting from catacomb to catacomb torso to torso skin to skin erasing past arrangements made on pocket maps the night-time dérive of a collector of street names the tomb raider of nomadic leavings or longings who frees you from familiar addresses safely stamped on the atlas of your mind the secondhand items no-one's ever owned it's not who runs or who desires snow slows you down the event is in the things escaping objects oscillating the contours of an unfound name and look the world blurs into dusk and the absent stand out like language suddenly palpable and snow just everywhere all elements carry the same heavy fog weight tons of smoke or ash say you could think with the mind of an hourglass the convex and concave forms of breathing you might go so far as to call it killing time

Post Scriptum on the Speed of Forgetting

Try to think of something conclusive, she urges. The swift detour people take, or the speed of their streamlined thoughts of departures. Of backdoors which suddenly swing open, the fearful speed with which an urban falcon twitches her head, the acceleration of summer, as it exits and leaves us with the terracotta floor of a dried up lake. Dead ducks in small heaps, cast-off clothing, a telegrammic beer bottle; the only convex items on the flat horizon after such a topographic stun. (Or the other way round. Think of the subliminal. The cowering dry grass knots, once overflowing litter bins shrinking, the decline of dehydrated willows, the concave, indifferent about duration; and below, the slow time of the sandclock's bulb.) And the timeless in between; the migrating swallows which after a long hour of silent gathering on electric wires cutting the continent in two exit history early morning without a hint or the smallest sound of the flap of a wing. And it is not a threat. The concave's bound to become convex. But if only you could think of a word with the race of light to forget the metropolis fast which, year after year, metamorphoses without you.

Joe Kennedy

Two Fallacies About Music Writing

It never occurred to me that I'd end up writing about music or, to formulate it a little differently, end up doing music writing. And maybe 'end up' is too emphatic, too terminal, for an activity I do in conjunction, and which is only incompletely commensurate, with what I *really do*. This latter point seems worth making inasmuch as what intrigues me more than any other aspect of the genre is the attendant suspicion that music writing is not something that anyone can *really do*, not only in the professional sense but also, and I think more significantly, in the existential one. I struggle to think of a category of journalism or, more narrowly, of cultural criticism which is regarded with more ceratopsid defensiveness as a violation of the intactness of the objects on which it comments and, in a way which contradicts but is not necessarily seen as incompatible with this, a vain and even impossible activity.

The latter objection to music writing lays claim to a defter catchphrase than the first. 'Writing [or even 'talking'] about music,' said Frank Zappa, or Elvis Costello, or Laurie Anderson, 'is like dancing about architecture - a really stupid thing to do.' It's not easy to tease out the precise meaning of this notion, but one might try. Apparently, it's reasonable to respond to one aesthetic medium using the idiom of another, but there are limits of propriety, and the (allegedly) non-verbal essence of music demands an identically extralingistic interpretation. I've always thought that this was idiot syllogism - is architecture, by implication a justifiable recipient of written attention, any less resistant to words? - but this is not my principle objection to the idea. The real problem is that the quip implies that the foremost obligation placed on any response to art is descriptive, in that it must hug the contours of a posited original. Dance is meant to do this to music. Good dancing is the corporealisation of music, a sequence of actions which gives the recording or performance physical coordinates; writing, on the other hand, lacks tools germane to the visceral petition of the sonic.

While the claim I'm going to make here is unlikely to be met sympathetically by those who insist that writing always falls short of the composition it supplicates to, it strikes me that what an evocative - and let's set aside for a moment the question of politicised criticism - music journalism does, and the reason it exists, is, precisely, anti-mimetic. Growing up in a small farming town which had much better access to the *NME* and *Melody Maker* than to record shops, my love of music germinated less in what I heard than in what I extrapolated from reviews. Articles about bands whose records I had little chance of buying, and whose shows I had no opportunity whatsoever to attend, produced fantasies which, in the complete unfeasibility of their verification, acted as provocations to establish a set of standards for music which sat at the limits of attainability. The 'lost chord' is one of pop and rock's most jarring clichés in a particular context - when I listen to *Dark Side of the Moon*, I don't perceive a band searching for it, but merely affecting such a search - but it gains more heft when applied to the pre-listener, the fan whose enthusiasm is based entirely on what is anticipated. One defence of music criticism positions it as a semi-autonomous artform whose parasitism can be forgiven. But what about the music which is conceived of in a way that is parasitic on criticism?

My guess is that a significant number of music critics write in the knowledge that a substantial portion of their audience might never hear, and might never even attempt to hear, what they're criticising. An extreme version of this occurs in accounts of music which simply does not exist. The most notable literary example of this is, of course, Vinteuil's sonata in Proust's *A la Recherche du Temps Perdu*. The manner in which this composition is evoked is one of the most powerful pieces of music writing in the archive, arguably because it emphasises the stubbornness the piece maintains in the face of any attempt at simple verbal equivalence:

> After a high note sustained through two whole bars, Swann sensed its approach, stealing forth from beneath that long-drawn sonority, stretched like a curtain of sound to veil the mystery of its incubation.

The 'in universe' power of the sonata lies in its inscrutability, and the appreciation of this (negative) quality is shunted from Swann to the reader. Reading this passage, Alex Ross - whose history of twentieth-century classical music *The Rest is Noise* can be enjoyed quite apart from any acquaintance with its subject - writes that 'Proust captures the imaginary dimension of musical experience'. While it might not be exactly what the critic is paid for, this 'imaginary dimension' is, I think, the place where a good number of people employed to write about music prefer to operate. Those who assert that music criticism fails because it is not the same thing as its object miss the point, because it is that very descriptive shortfall which gives criticism its autonomous aesthetic potency.

Parallel to the mimetic fallacy is the belief that music writers, by suggesting historical and political contexts, intrude upon an intimate encounter between listener and composition which should, for reasons which are never really made clear, remain sacrosanct. Publishing music journalism online has opened me to this indictment frequently in the form of the below-the-line comment. One I'll never forget, and I see no reason to say which album I was reviewing when I attracted this remark, was 'For God's sake, concentrate on the music, not the contents of your own mind'. The note of desperation struck by this plea is, and I don't think it's extreme to make this point, an indication of the purchase obtained by one of the fundamental tenets of neoliberal ideology in terms of its relation to culture, namely that aesthetic objects be seen as sui generis, securely individual and therefore easy to 'cleanly' commodify. Obviously, ideology being impersonal, I'm not saying that this was at the forefront of the commenter's mind, but there has been a deep internalisation of the idea that linking art to politics *in any way whatsoever* is somehow transgressive.

Emerging from this is a fantasy that somehow music can be written about without recourse to any external referent, although the political 'outside' is what is viewed as most unclean. But, even if I or any other critic had the inclination to do this, where would such an ascetic language come from? And would I not once again come up against the problem that music eludes mimesis? The lure of 'imaginary' music, for me, lay in the way that the writers I looked up to as a teenager (and, in fact, now) captured that 'dimension' but also mapped its extensions, its capacity to respond to non-musical circumstances and effect change in the world. What could be more enthralling than the hypothesising of a revolutionary music which, in its failure to come to fruition, constantly pulls us onwards in a spirit of restless intrigue?

Plainly, few things are more thrilling and innervating than finding a piece of music which comes close to fulfilling these conditions - I'm currently listening to Art Ensemble of Chicago's 'Theme de Yoyo', which almost does so for me - but there's also a strange moment of disappointment in their discovery, as if our libido has been arrested and reminded of its own finitude. As an answer to the grievances many hold music journalists to account for, one might say that, on good form, they produce writing which hooks desire and leads it on, leaving it always partially unfulfilled.

Kathryn Gray

Salad Days

I must confess that, right back at the beginning, becoming a poet had never been design. It was pure, happy accident. I had planned originally to embark on a fiction writing course in the evenings. I had arrived in London a troubled soul - and a refugee from an abandoned career path as a Medievalist. I required something to refuel my ambition - not simply for some sort of career, whatever that meant - but, in truth, for life itself. At 25, after years of perfectionist striving for validation through academic achievement that had seemingly come to nought, I felt washed up. So I would reinvent myself and redirect that struggle. But the course I had planned to do was full - everyone has a novel in them, it would seem. There was, however, one place - *one place* - on a poetry writing course with Michael Donaghy. The late, great Michael Donaghy. I could not have known then that the experience would redefine my entire life after; I was unfamiliar with his work, but I liked his name. Donaghy was not merely a master craftsman, a brilliant man of exceedingly good taste, he was also, for his students, an Obi-Wan Kenobi of sorts. A touchstone of what it meant to be a poet. A shepherd, a philosopher. When he first entered the classroom, that Thursday evening just over 15 years ago, I had met my future.

Why is this relevant? I've been thinking a lot about the matter of 'making it' as a poet lately. There's an official term for it: emergence. Within emergence, there are many stages, from first publication in a small 'zine, for example, to the very heights of exposure - winning an impressive array of awards, permeating the wider culture, and perhaps, even, presenting a BBC programme for radio or television on poetry. Many will know the first stage; few will ever come close to the last. Yes, I've been thinking about emergence. How younger, new poets are making their way forward now. What it all adds up to. How I came to be where I am.

Back then, in the late 1990s, to get ahead in poetry, the rules of the game seemed clear enough. You had a list of magazines to send to, compiled from the acknowledgements pages of successful collections. You waited patiently for the rejection slips, which surely came, dependable as the weather. You applied for an Eric Gregory. You maybe received an Eric Gregory. You tried those same magazines again and this time, maybe, the editors, convinced by the external validation of the Gregory or maybe - even without a Gregory - the fact that you'd come back two years later, and better, said yes. You perhaps approached a leading publisher. The editor romanced you briefly, but ultimately turned you down. You weren't for them.

You continued to attend open mic nights. You tried to recite your work by heart and occasionally forgot your own words. Then, maybe, you got lucky and a small press approached you. Or you sent in your manuscript, a covering letter detailing your commitment... And... Congratulations. You have officially arrived. Welcome, minor poet!

But, over the past fifteen years, I've watched things change. I detect greater dissatisfaction from young poets coming up through the ranks now. They question the preeminence of the major commercial presses. They increasingly question the established magazine culture - where such still exists. There are poets organizing readings in London - though how much of this amounts to an internal conversation, not dissimilar to that of the academic milieu, remains a moot point. But in an age of recession and a shrinking readership,[1] there's a sense of entrepreneurial Blitz spirit out there. There are some good small presses run by younger poets - Nine Arches and Sidekick Books being two I especially admire. And the internet has afforded possibilities. There are fine online magazines such as *Sabotage*, a pamphlet reviews site run by a young and passionate crew, and *Poems in Which*, edited by Amy Key and Nia Davies, the incoming editor of *Poetry Wales*. Sometimes, in my moments of feeling absolutely ancient and conservative, I wonder why my generation didn't pursue such interesting avenues. Particularly as they are borne of a spirit of community. But the internet was different then, and we had the game with its rules, which was very comforting, even as it was periodically soul-destroying. More recent generations have been less keen to put up and shut up - and I've watched these talented upstarts with not a little envy. This, I remind myself, is both the great lesson and sorrow of the ageing process. However, for all that this activity is highly commendable, hanging over it is the sense that, in their desire to achieve, and achieve *young*, they are not so very different from my generation.

For the world from whence I sprang was still coasting the wave of 1994's New Gen Poets - a selection of twenty hip young gun-slinging poets under forty. There had been then perhaps an optimistic belief that contemporary poetry could triumph over its diminished audience and its lack of critical scrutiny through marketing. There were many brilliant poets among that 1994 cohort - Donaghy himself was one - and many of those figures remain important to me. But for those generations which followed them there was perhaps the sense in which we were stepping into other people's clothes. Yes, in the stylistic sense - the New Gen influence remains palpable even now. But there was something more again. The sense that we consciously attempted to replicate their apparently neat journey - the Gregory awards, publication in the very same aspirational journals credited in their acknowledgements pages, residency in London if possible - and that we felt that we, too, might acquire some of their gilt and promotion. We simply had to be well behaved. Of course, they themselves were not so, but, crucially, they were packaged as such - each a coherent

1. As suggested, in no small part, by Nielsen BookScan data over the last three years, showing most recently, a fall of 18.5% volume of sales and 15.9% in value.

narrative of glittering, new success. They became the rule. Ten years on, however, its sequel, Next Gen, sank like the proverbial stone as a promotion, for all the greatly accomplished poets included in it. The world had changed. Marketing had not increased the commercial dimensions of the scene. And marketing was no substitute for deep engagement.

And frustrations had built up by then. The poetry world was jaded. Lists were slowing their rate of signings. And in several cases it seems to me now that they were radically behind the times in recognizing the potential of fresh talent - particularly the commercials (though they now seem to be catching up). UK poetry awards culture, birthed in the early 1990s, had proved the status of the publisher as much, arguably, as a poet's unique achievement. Over time, this led to increased and enduring skepticism and disenchantment. Smaller magazines, as always beset by poetry's fragile ecosystem, had folded or gone into a lengthy hiatus - but many were never replaced by new platforms. Pressure only increased on the pages of the most elite journals - which have always, of course, proved to be the most elusive gains.

Perhaps in no small part due to creative writing degrees, poet advocacy seems to have strengthened over the years - and expectations may have heightened more generally as a result. It is now not unsurprising to pick up a new collection from a poet and find that their publication track record is not the lengthy roll-call it would have been of old. Sometimes there is barely any to speak of. It can occasionally be misleading to younger poets outside of this milieu. Senior poets directly recommend to editors and magazine editors or are willing to provide endorsement, and there is a sense of talent scouting and fostering on a scale not previously seen, even if it was always rather irregularly present. And in my former life as a magazine editor (at *New Welsh Review*, from 2008 to 2011), I was often surprised at how many covering letters placed great emphasis on the fact that the poet was studying for an MA in creative writing. There was a sense, increasingly, that new poets saw the creative writing degree itself as a tangible 'emergence factor' or credit to be taken into consideration. (It wasn't, and I didn't, I hasten to add.) But it was fascinating to note this belief in new poets studying on such programmes.

Creative writing degrees have of course sprung up everywhere. I have to say that I could count a number of important younger poets - some of my favourites - who have taken this route. But I am troubled by the increasing belief on the part of aspiring poets that it's a necessary one. If a year or more of concentrated focus within a community of writers is what you're seeking, then an MA is certainly desirable over the evening-class workshop route. But sometimes I wonder how healthy it is for poets to study on courses alongside fictioneers who, despite their own economic vicissitudes and competition within the field, possess commercial dimensions and potential to their work which are simply unavailable to poets. The first rule of poetry is to expect nothing material of it. It will bring you no riches and little glory. Although, in my day, I thought I would buck this trend.

Yes, I do worry about expectation.

Salt Publishing's mothballing of its poetry operations earlier this year was indeed a sad move, as Clare Pollard recently noted in a characteristically wise and engaged post on her blog.[2] I've admired many poets on its list. And the acquisition of Roddy Lumsden as editor in recent years was an inspired choice. Lumsden is a man with an encyclopedic knowledge of Anglophone poetry, both that of the UK and the US. He is a talented editor, as well as an accomplished poet in his own right, who brings out the best in younger poets. Previous to his recruitment, however, the Salt list betrayed a lack of editorial intervention. And Salt published simply too much - a familiar argument that I do not need to rehearse here. A number of collections I had read seemed to me to amount to not so much a failure of talent but of a prematurity in design. And yet those poets rushed towards print. Why?

It was not so long ago that poets toiled long in the dark and demoralizing hinterland of unpaid poetry readings and rejection slips. It was seen as a necessary part of the apprenticeship. It was not uncommon to encounter talented poets who were ten years into their writing and had yet to hold their own book in their hands. They were still relatively cheerful, hopeful, motivated. And I admired them, even as I was certain I didn't want to *be* one. As the acceptance letters began to arrive for me, from all the right places, and as I plotted each new move towards book publication, I felt I knew better than them. There have always been, of course, outlier poets who - due to chance or excellence or a combination of the two - emerge quickly and efficiently from their beginnings. But now, I feel, there is the sense everywhere that the desire to emerge seems, very frequently, to take priority over the actual development of talent - so that the patient *and* talented seem to be something of a dying breed. A belief that if you don't land immediately onto the poetry scene with fireworks then you are a tired, unwanted thing. If that means you are all the more in potential rather than proven, then so be it.

Perhaps the very fact of poetry's non-commercial dimension and the subsidy culture supporting it has been the great enemy of patience in this regard. With readerships only continuing to shrink, perhaps in some subtle and not-so-subtle ways there is a sense that no one needs to *hotly* anticipate your first collection, for there is the worrying notion - which we must push hastily to the back of our minds - that there may be no one there to open its pages in any case, hotly or otherwise. The pressure to publish for a new poet now is tremendous - and that even relates to simply placing individual poems. Visibility, any visibility, seems to matter, and I increasingly wonder how much this may in fact account for the recent plagiarism scandal. Perhaps an over-anxious desire for visibility on the part of practitioners naturally follows from poetry's predicament - we are talking about an art form which has largely slipped from view in the public imagination. There is less winnowing

2. http://clarepollard.wordpress.com/2013/05/20/the-health-of-poetry/

and affirmation available to many aspiring poets. And with good poets often going largely unnoticed even if they do secure publication, it can be hard to contextualize yourself if you are, in fact, an unready poet. After all, what's the difference in selling ninety copies or three hundred? It's all pretty much peanuts. What does achievement mean, anyhow? Shouldn't young poets just 'get out there'? That is certainly what I thought - once.

For at least twenty years now, poetry has been on the verge of apocalypse. It's a popular sound bite. Poetry criticism - written, as most of it is, by us poets with our frequently inescapable conflicts of interest - is in a bad way. There is difficulty in tackling major names and, potentially, the defects of their work. 'Prestige' coverage in the broadsheets is scant and, where such exists, is largely centred around the major commercial publishers and their more established names - typically served with more praise than pedantry. Magazines, negotiating the high volume of titles requiring consideration, have frequently little choice but to offer scrutiny - most particularly of newer poets - through round-up reviews, which can often result in a title receiving little more than a few hundred words of notice, and sometimes less. The balance of reflecting the status quo of the poetry world and challenging it through the reviews pages, in terms of which poets you select for coverage and as to what amount of space you allot them, remains an enduring problem for editors, as I myself know from experience. With most print magazines within the poetry world subject to remit and sales targets laid down by their funding bodies, and in a hostile economic climate which recommends caution over daring, it can be surprisingly difficult to present one's own, true vision as an editor or reassessments of the scene. But without such autonomy very little can or does change or improve. Someone recently drew my attention to a great quote from the Scottish supremo Douglas Dunn: 'An honest, descriptive, detailed, clarifying criticism keeps poetry healthy - it's poetry's weedkiller and, to the extent it encourages what's best in writing, it can nourish poetry too. No good growth without good gardeners.' Thin critical culture across the board is weakening the critical faculties and context of poets themselves.

Awards culture has become not merely a marketing tool but, apparently, an arbiter of taste. It is difficult to understand a poet's achievement outside of awards culture. And then, poetry is an art form at odds with twenty-four-hour rolling news culture, a preoccupation with the ephemeral, the Total Noise. Yet so much of what is now being written seems to me to be too eager to adapt itself to that culture rather than to do what poetry is best placed to do - engage against it. Quirky narratives, monologues by inanimate objects, telling-it-slant-with-a-wink lyrics are everywhere. Irony is increasingly not particularly clever or novel, but a near-exhausted mode. (I confess I, too, have sinned.) Individual poetic identity seems to have been diluted. There is more assimilation than distinctiveness. At *New Welsh Review*, it was often hard to find a unique voice among the submissions pile. So many poems, by apparently different people, seemed to share the same DNA. Again, I think awards culture has much to answer for. Well-meaning though it undoubtedly is, it often achieves the very opposite of fine criticism - by encouraging replication rather than praising innovation and lambasting the typical.

Perhaps the key task for young poets is to move away from the preoccupation with emergence. To resist publication over practice. To resist packaging. To resist that death of all ambition - which is, paradoxically, the temptation of acclaim. But it is a complex matter now to understand oneself as a poet before one has a platform, and it is also a bold gamble, involving patience, time, a deep commitment to craft. A bold gamble I was not prepared to take - much to my regret.

My own story as a poet requires a little fleshing out for context. And so I found myself in Donaghy's poetry workshops. *Serendipity*. Salad days. But what followed was all too intentional and all too focused on emergence rather than apprenticeship. My path to publication was relatively swift. My book received, by luck (because, you know, it really is luck), a few nominations. It is easy, of course, to say that such things mean little when you have actually been fortunate enough to experience them. So I won't lie. I enjoyed it all, at the time; I was grateful. I had travelled far. But I was unready. It resulted in years of silence. And it certainly came at the cost of a better book - and a better poet.

Interview

Meirion Jordan Interviews Jim Goar

This interview is part of a collaborative conversation, not only between two poets but between *Lighthouse* and *The Volta* (http://www.thevolta.org). The second part, where Jim Goar interviews Meirion Jordan, will appear in a Spring issue of *The Volta*, along with links to the *Lighthouse* blog where this piece will be reproduced for our online readers.

Meirion Jordan: By way of introducing yourself a little, can you tell us something about how you started writing poetry? What are you most proud of about your career so far? And what do you think are the most important milestones in the life of a young poet?

Jim Goar: I came to poetry pretty late. I only began to take it seriously when I was living in China in 1999/2000. I felt I was seeing something new and poetry was a way to express it. I'm not sure about milestones, but for me, *Whole Milk*, written at the end of my MFA study, was the first time that I knew what I was doing. Something just clicked and I was very much in the middle of it as it was occurring; I was certain of it. Maybe a milestone is that moment, after years of apprenticing, when you feel like you've lost the tutor.

MJ: Speaking of milestones, you've been published in the US and in the UK, and you studied for your PhD in the UK as well. Do you think there's any difference between the poetry readerships between those two countries? How do their differences manifest themselves?

JG: I don't know that I'd place the divide along national boundaries but one of taste. The readership for award presses are not the same as the readers of innovative poetry. There is overlap, but not much. The award presses in the UK would find more familiar relations in the award presses in the States than with their innovative peers in the UK. The problem then is alerting the reader who enjoys the award press in the States that there is an award press in the UK. With this in mind, I'm not really sure that there is that much difference in readership taste, just in getting them the goods.

MJ: As someone who has worked on both sides of the publishing/writing divide, then, how do you think those goods should be delivered? Should poets be doing more to alert poetry readerships as to what takes place on the other side of the Atlantic?

JG: The shipping cost seems to be what is most prohibitive. It costs too much for most publishers in the UK to send their books to SPD. And, in the UK, while there are distributers for small publishers, there is nothing so central as SPD. So, even if the US publisher wishes to spend the money on shipping, who should they ship it to? To cut international shipping costs, maybe more presses could use POD for their books not distributed in their home country.

MJ: While we're on the subject of national boundaries, it seems to me that your poetry works a great deal on the interface between landscape and history. Some of your poems in *The Louisiana Purchase* and *The Dustbowl* in particular appear to read one for the other. How do you see these relationships in your work? Would you say that poetry is particularly well suited to such re-markings of boundaries and re-drawings of maps?

JG: Landscape and history are intimately tied. There needs to be someone over the river so I can write my history. We are always in conversation with our bounds, or, more often, the bounds are at work on us. The bounds we define and/or accept define us and our neighbor. My poetry, I think, continually attempts to know what and why is around and inside of me. Instead of Sunday school, I had Disney and baseball. I want to know how these and other givens come at me. What do they carry with them? What is mine and where do I begin? What is this construct? And, for me, poetry is the only tool I have that can do this. I am able to push on language with the language I am given.

MJ: Doesn't this place your poetry alongside the rather earthy tradition of Heaney, Hughes, and Hill, then? If poetry is a tool, and language a given, how far away are you from Heaney's digging pen, or Hill's coin hoards that mirror his hoarded words? Or does this relationship with language work very differently if your poetry-tools are Saturday-morning cartoons and trash-cans the morning after the Yankees game?

JG: If given is something like an ideology, then yes, we are it without noticing. Language is not something we put our thoughts into, it is our thoughts. We are this thing, but what this thing is and why and for what remains unknown. The topic of the poem, for example baseball or legend, is a façade that provides a texture through which a more important exploration can occur. Breton points to the trash bin when he states that 'we, who have made no effort whatsoever to filter, who in our works have made ourselves into simple receptacles of so many echoes.' While there might be a way to filter the content, language is unfilterable. We can dig through the trash bin, either filtering the content or not filtering the content, but that is not the thing; language adheres more than words. Poetry allows an engagement with this always hidden and resistant language. I'm not well enough acquainted with Heaney, Hughes or Hill to respond to their earthy tradition. Does their poetry engage in process like compost? Are they in the mix?

MJ: You wrote part of your PhD on the poetry of Jack Spicer, and *The Dustbowl* in particular carries a great deal of influence from his work. What do you find to be most important, or powerful, in Spicer's work, and how has Spicer's influence made itself felt for you? What advice would you give on balancing an acknowledgment of our debts to other poets against keeping your writing feeling fresh?

JG: The walls of Spicer's poetry are porous. Each poem talks to other poems. I don't believe there is a single Spicer poem that you could hold up and say that this is great. It is the poems' interstices, these creeping and always forming alleyways for connections that attract and involve me. I feel necessary in the making of his poems more than I do with any other poet I've read. His poems welcome my voice as they welcome the alien's. The debt is in the impetus to write, but in the actual writing, what I learned from Spicer is that I don't owe him anything and the poems I write don't owe me anything.

MJ: Memorably, Spicer described *The Holy Grail* as 'the opposite of poetry'. How do you think writing Arthurian poetry challenges our ideas of what should be, or what should be in, poetry?

JG: *The Holy Grail* was not a book about Arthur or the Grail. Instead, Spicer used these stories as a screen through which he could not see. By writing through the Grail legend he was able to further distance himself from the poem in composition and let the outside work through him. Of course, this attempt to keep himself out of it was not completely successful. The poems of *The Holy Grail* are a recounting of this struggle between Spicer and the outside for command of the poem. This was the battle, the quest, the poem itself was the Grail struggle.

I don't think then that it matters much what we write through. Arthurian legend is a great tool because there is so much of it. The repetitive narrative of the impossibility of Gawain's quest or the almost impossibility of Percival's or the inevitability of the non-human Galahad, play out again and again over the centuries. There is so much fodder for the outside to work with. That said, I'm not sure what could be excluded from poetry or why it should be excluded. What is marked by absence? Sherlock Holmes was curious about the dog that did not bark.

MJ: Where do you think you engage with the idea of Arthur? Does Arthur represent a point of contact with a particular poetic tradition, or a touchstone for what you see as being important in your work?

JG: More than Arthur, I was interested in the questing knights. I liked their human characteristics that kept them from the Grail. I liked how even though author after author sent them out on these impossible errands, they kept going and they did it with a straight face. They tried for the Grail. I appreciate this attempt, this impossible struggle.

MJ: I'm interested that you find that the knights are a more productive focus, which seems to connect with how you read the landscapes of your poems. I was particularly struck by:

> Left Ireland for
> Iceland for a tropical island. Grew
> the sword from a rubber tree. Pulled
> but Elaine held tight. The same old song.
> In a magical stutter. Galahad was born.

Do you think that in *The Dustbowl* you've connected with the heroic geography of these medieval stories, where the landscape almost grows into vision in response to the hero's internal, perhaps impossible, spiritual difficulties?

JG: I entered the Grail legend through Spicer. I wanted to know at what points his Grail legend touched the ones that preceded it. At that time I was treating Spicer's Grail as though it were situated firmly within the tradition. So, reading legend after legend, and seeing these connections not only to Spicer, but of course, to the other versions of the legend, the narrative changed from quest to farce. The Grail did not serve these knights, these knights served the author. The various authors moved them this way and that. In the Green Knight, it was a setup from the start, a kind of parlor game. What the uninitiated reader thought was a real adventure turns out to be a test which Gawain has failed. Bercilak, his host, who was also the Green Knight, explains himself thus: 'She sent me off in that form to your noble hall / To put its pride to the proof and see whether they were true, / The great things that were told of the Round Table' (Merwin 2004, 167). In the end, after this great and intricate story, we see that it has all been a ruse concocted by Arthur's sister, Morgan Le Fey. Gawain, as was his fate in these legends, was bound to lose; how much of this was Gawain aware of? As far as geographies, Spicer makes an interesting point in his fifth poem of Gawain: 'On the sea / (There is never an ocean in all Grail Legend)'. In Malory's *Le Morte Darthur*, there are numerous mentions of sea, but not a single mention of ocean. Tennyson, on the other hand, adds an ocean to the Arthurian legend. He writes, 'On one side lay the Ocean, and on one / Lay a great water, and the moon was full' (1983, 292). Geographies are in play as well. There is a shifting under the feet of the knight. And, as Lady Bercilak was aware of Gawain's past, so Gawain must have an awareness of his past beyond the book (did he know he had no chance?); I wanted it all to be in play. I wanted knights that knew and could comment on their fate, knights that no longer had to play the same game. I wanted to resituate them, to give them another chance at a new kind of failure, something in which they were a part, something more human.

MJ: In much of your work you use very tight, compacted verse structures - *Dustbowl* in particular comes to mind with its square verses like little plots of land. But in *Seoul Bus Poems* it looks like you needed to take up more of the page, to open the verse out; what was it about the poems that made you want to capture a new sort of relationship with the space of the page? Do you think you'll revisit that relationship?

JG: *Seoul Bus Poems* occurred while my language was very much in transition. I was teaching English as a Second Language in Seoul, so my thoughts and what I was hearing and producing were not linked in the way that they had been before. There was air in the attempts to find footholds in language. I think that play of unsettled thought needed space on the page. I'd like to revisit the space, but I can't find the justification. The more recent drafts I'd made in that form felt forced and so I began to squeeze them into constraints. In fact, the newest series is even tighter than *The Dustbowl*. I'm building walls of words in the hopes of turning spectacle back on itself. Maybe tomorrow it will be different.

MJ: One final question. You've taken the time to produce your own journal in the past. How did you find the experience? What lessons do you think it taught you about how people make, print, or consume poetry? Do you think it brought about any changes in your writing?

JG: I began *past simple* while I was living in Seoul. I did not have ready access to print journals, so my readings were mostly digital. After getting an idea of what was out there, I wanted to join the conversation. Mostly, I wanted to read what I wanted to read and to see if likeminded people would enter unexpectedly. Editing a journal put more work in front of me, so yes, my work changed through it. For the most part, I really enjoyed it. I was introduced to new poets and it was a way for me to reach out to poets that I respected. As far as consumption, I'm not really sure. These days, even though I am back in the States, most of my reading is done on my computer. When I read I also write so the transition is faster and more connected that way. That is how I'm consuming today, but who knows about tomorrow.

Author Biographies

Vish Amarasinghe studies English at Aberystwyth University, and keenly pursues musical interests.

James Coghill feels slightly dubious about everything and does not know why. He has been published in *Popshot Magazine*, *The Cadaverine*, *Orbis*, and *Acumen*. He loves all things strange and animal-related.

Melissa Diem is a widely published poet and writer. Her poetry films have been screened in many countries.

Ian Duhig has written six books of poetry, most recently *Pandorama* (Picador, 2010), and was chair of the judges for this year's T S Eliot prize. He is currently engaged in the Digressions project based around Shandy Hall and will be publishing a chapbook called *Digressions* with Smokestack this year.

Francine Elena has recently had poems published by *Best British Poetry* 2013, *The Quietus* and *Clinic*. Her chapbook *Christmas Lantern* is published by 3AM Press. @FrancineElena

Imogen Forster translates fiction and art history from French, Spanish, Italian and Catalan. Her poems appear online and on paper.

Jim Goar was born in San Francisco, California and grew up in Tucson, Arizona. He studied at the University of Arizona, Naropa University, and, most recently, the University of East Anglia. He is the author of *Seoul Bus Poems* (Reality Street, 2010), *The Louisiana Purchase* (Rose Metal Press, 2011), *The Dustbowl* (Shearsman Books, 2014) and the chapbook, *Whole Milk* (Effing Press, 2006).

Kathryn Gray is a poet and a former editor of both the *New Welsh Review* and Parthian Books. Her first collection of poetry, *The Never Never* (Seren, 2004) was shortlisted for the T S Eliot prize. She is currently part of the Devolved Voices project, examining emergence in contemporary Welsh poetry.

Matt Howard is 35 and lives in Norwich and works for the RSPB. Matt has had poems in several magazines including current issues of *The Rialto* and *The North*. He was selected as one of the participants in this year's Aldeburgh Poetry Festival Masterclass.

Joe Kennedy is a writer and lecturer based in London. He has taught English and cultural theory at the universities of East Anglia, Portsmouth, Brighton and Sussex, and his writing on music, literature and sport has appeared in publications such as *The Quietus*, *The Times Literary Supplement* and *When Saturday Comes*.

Agnes Lehoczky is a Hungarian-born poet, scholar and translator. She has published two collections of poetry in English, *Budapest to Babel* (2008) and *Rememberer* (2012) by Egg Box Publishing. She was Hungary's representative for Poetry Parnassus at Southbank Centre in Summer 2012. Her third collection, *Carillonneur*, is out by Shearsman in April 2014. She currently works as a lecturer at the University of Sheffield.

Manuela Moser is currently a postgraduate student in the Seamus Heaney Centre for Poetry. She co-runs The Lifeboat reading series.

Duran Parsi has always been an avid reader and writer of poetry since college and draws influence from Beat generation poets.

Eleanor Perry is a poet, PhD student and co-editor of *ZONE* magazine.

Simon Petkovich is a published Australian poet who is married and with his wife and two sons lives in Melbourne.

Jack Reynolds is from Lowestoft.

Andrew Spragg lives in London. Recent books include *To Blart & Kid* (Like This Press, 2013) and *A Treatise on Disaster* (Contraband Books, 2013). There are others.

Christopher Tracy works as a library assistant. He is a UEA history graduate, and oversees the Poetry Unbound project at the Norfolk and Norwich Millennium Library, where he also acts as a union steward.

Lara Williams is a writer based in Manchester. She has just completed a Creative Writing MA at Manchester Metropolitan University. She works in Digital Media. larawilliams.wordpress.com

Lighthouse

a literary journal for new writing

Ethos

Lighthouse is aimed a new writing primarily (but not exclusively) emerging from the UK writing scene. We are particularly interested in seeing the experimental as well as the traditional. We are published by Gatehouse Press, an award-winning independent press set for new writing. We run on a voluntary basis and are not-for-profit. All money made is reinvested in future publications.

***Lighthouse* on the Internet**
gatehousepress.com/lighthouse

Follow us on Twitter
@lighthouseJrnl

Facebook
Lighthouse Literary Journal

SUBSCRIBE TO LIGHTHOUSE

Lighthouse is a new journal published three times per year to give space and support to new talent. We look to publish the best short fiction and poetry emerging from the UK writing scene.

1 year	**2 years**
£18.00 (£4.50 per copy)	£32.00 (£4.00 per copy)
Saving 50p per issue	Saving £1.00 per issue

SUBMIT YOUR WORK

We're currently accepting short fiction, poetry and artwork submissions, so if you'd like your work featured in the next issue, go to

www.gatehousepress.com/lighthouse